Sudden Spring

by Muriel, the Marquise de Chambrun

designed by Dorothy Peebles

Colors on the Hill

Shapes Against the Sky

Faces of Time

I Know Your Love

The C. R. Gibson Company, Publishers
Norwalk, Connecticut

To Jean Pierre, my husband

*Grateful acknowledgment is made to the
University of Cincinnati to reprint selections from
Salisbury Cathedral and Other Poems by Muriel,
the Marquise de Chambrun*

Colors on the Hill

Colors on the Hill

I speak to you
Of colors on the hill,
A distant mottled sky,
The muddied swirling river-whirl
That separates the states,
And spill of gold
Upon the rusted evening trees
I speak ... I speak of these.
I watch
While ghosted building blocks float
In the later grey-and-gathering mists
Here now; then gone;
Then back again
Forlorn in man-made sulphured veils
All opalled as the evening rides
I speak ... I speak of these.
I speak to you
Of blueness of the night
Of hills now velvet dark
Of city spread
With myriad of flashing, garish-lights,
Of better diamonds in the firmament
They: still and quiet in silver frosted
                    breeze
I speak ... I speak of these.

Night Storm

In bed, womb-warm,
I listen to the outside storm
And to the beam-creaked sounds within...
Shifting shadows trace the room;
Branches rasp and scrape against
The worn brick walls;
And, above the roar,
I hear the shivering sighs
And calls
Of wind-tossed willow
As it lifts and flies...
And falls.

Listen

Take time out, my friend, to listen to life
Hear the wind whispering secrets in the trees
Tune in to the symphony of living
Listen to the varied calls of birds
The rush of water over sunlit rocks
River sounds
Splash of a leaping fish
Rhapsody of buzzing insects
The drone of many a bee
And full orchestra of flying sounds
Hush; Now can you hear
The slithering snake
Making its stealthy way to the water's edge
Passing over brittle twig and leaf?

The unwarned placid warbled croak
        of emerald frog
Singing among the wind-stirred reeds?
And, soft as a sigh, the faintest hum as
Glittering waterbug skims the river?

Sudden Spring

When gilded head of crocus breaks the earth
And blossom trembles on the almond tree
The sun is warmer on my aging back
And memories come crowding in to me
I find a sudden spring.

The dragging winter months have lasted long
And chill has kept me prisoned at my hearth
My senses dulled by many months disuse
But suddenly it is spring again!

With eagerness I daily search them out:
Remembered signs and joys returned
The first dark hidden violet;
The bursting gold of daffodil,
The early song of finch upon the bough
The scarlet flash of cardinal
And I am young again
Because
I find a sudden spring.

After Rain

How fresh the garden after rain!
The pungent scent of loamy earth all wet
Raindrops which glister on the oranged velvet
Of the proud wallflower
And there the blackbird walks insolent
On yellow legs
His polished beak pulling worms
From rich black beds
And flinging brittle snails against
The candy-tufted paves.

Blue

Blue against blue against blue
Misted lilac behind the purple hollyhock
Deep violets in a shaded place
Wisteria on a slated wall
Grey-blue rocks set in a hazy sea
Shaded from vivid blue to blue
Stretched to a windwashed sky
Paling into infinity.
Blue striking on the sharp blue-whiteness
Of my sunlit home
All blue beyond;
And framed with sea and sky,
The best of all —
The blue-drenched blossom
                of the jacaranda trees!

Essence of an Orchard

Breathe the appled-air
It seeps throughout the house —
From under eaves,
In attics where the pippins are stored;
From the cellars where dusted barrels
Are cider-rich and sharper apples
Lie in cool green rows
All freckle-sprayed —
And even the leather-tooled books
In the library
Smell of the appled-air
And faded cretonned chairs
Have absorbed the scent.

The Hawk

The wind gives tides to the grasses
And the hawk matches his eye
To movements of life
Weeding the seething green.
His descent is sudden
And as relentless
And sure as a dropped stone.

Watermelon Days

Thoughts hang heavy
Like the Spanish Moss which drapes the choking
trees

These are the Watermelon Days
Yawned-away time;
Rocked-away hours—
Listening to the persistent call of heat bird
In monotone
And down in the arched mangroves
A thousand bullfrogs throb
In comfortable humidity.

I need the Sea

Like some sea-creature I am always called
By the beating sound of the surf
And, homing, breathe the salt on the wind
Walking mile upon mile on silvered stretch
                    of beach
Feeling the shifting patterned wetness
                    underfoot
Searching amid the bounty of sea-jewels
Cast upon the shore
For pearly mauve and pink of shell
                    or vivid-prickled
Urchin;
Savouring the almost sensual tang
                    of tarred net
These things I love and need.
It matters not to me the season
Nor the varied mood;
Warm, calm or chopping-blue
Or chilled and metalled grey
Each changing facet of the sea
Is like a miracle.

Shapes Against the Sky

The Algarve

I know a hill
Where clapping black bird laughs
And scent of wild fig
Is lifted by the wind
To blend with breath of herbs
That tuft the jagged edge
Of ravined rocks.
And we have found this hill
Where sleepy donkeys
Patch the thorny sweeps
And, striped and honeyed-fat,
The yellow-dusted bumblebee
Treads from a rose
And lifts its heavy, velvet-self
Into the sun-dried air.

And there we lie
Absorbing sun and silence on our hill
Forgetting other worlds.
Below: a valley rich with vine,
                with nut and fig.
Beyond: the spreading, changing sea.
Above: the cloudless bowl of air.
Where clapping black bird laughs.

Night in Portugal

The half moon rests:
A gilded harp
On frail gauze of cloud;
The sea swallows its reflections —
And the vast dark heavens
Have no margin
For the stars
Have joined
The lights of the fishing boats.

Dawn in Xaun

One dawn in Xaun we climbed a stony hill
Still heavy-eyed with sleep
Past mountain waterfall bubbling down in
Dappled brook
Carrying water to the darkened town
Awakening now, lantern by lantern, with the call
Of the faithful from the minaret
Echoing across still purpled valleys.
10 *We sat, knees clasp't, and watched*
The brilliant orb that was the sun
Rise from its hidden bed behind the hills
Filling the bowl with stretching dawn
Lighting the crystalled grass.

Highland Night

How many times
Across great stone walls
Did the wind sing
Its wild songs,
And carry the screams
Of the bagpipes
To rake the cold-starred night
Which lidded
The humped shadows of hills,
Dim in cast silver,
Where darkened heather slept?
And how many nights
Did your long, thistle-silk hair
Join the wind
And touch my face?

On Scottish Moorland

On heathered bank I lie
Eyes closed to scurrying clouds
Hands flat against the warm scratched green
And open book aside
Its pages turning in the quickening breeze
For I want nothing but this peace
The scent of it
The feel
I do not even want the muted colors
That await my lidded eyes.

Autumn in England

I walked in autumn
Watched the leaves drift down
From lofty parent trees
A brilliant colored rain of crimson,
                    gold and flame
The crackling carpet made around my feet.
The air, now nipped with winter's
                    first dire chill,
Brought to my cheeks a glow.

I saw a hare's white scut
Fast — fast
Across the rich tilled earth of Kent
And now I held my breath:
The old red fox, more russet than the earth,
I saw him, too.

I reached the silent pond
Cold, deep and grey and still
With willow trailing in its glassy depth
The sad pale weeping boughs

And as I trod the wild duck took wing
With startled cry
Into the darkening sky.

Across the meadows far
I saw the distant thatch of Tudor manor home
Its mellowed chimney bricks issuing smoke
Which called me back for tea
                    before logged fire

Where heavy velvet drapes
Closed out the autumn eve
I'd sip, from flowered china cup,
The sweet warm brew.

Salisbury Cathedral

Through Gothic archway
Under gargoyled eaves
Shared afternoon
Remember?
Chilled by the air of centuries gone
We walked
Echoed by our footfalls
On time-polished stone
Breathed the mustiness
Of history
Saw the noseless knights
Lying coupled in eternity
With their pitted, unloved wives
Blinded by the sunlight as we left
We looked up high
At the moving slender spire
Of the Lady of Cathedrals.

Languedoc

I will try to press upon your eyes
A picture of an ochred part of France
South, wrapped in sheltered shadow of
The Pyrenees:

The ancient heart of Languedoc.
There you will find that special
                palest faded brick
Which built the spreading châteaux
                of the land
And tiny, pink-hued hamlets raise
Their haunted turrets to the sky
Caught nestled in an ambered light
Where grapes pour forth their vintaged blood.
It seems that peace of centuries
                has drenched this earth
Forgetting now the wars which bruised
                and crushed
The rambling rose of France
Which clings with renewed strength
                on mellowed walls
And earth, the skies, the very air
Seem coralled in eternity.

Faces of Time

The Berber Boy

His reeded music rose from whence he lay
Wrapped in his homespun cloak
Of coarse brown wool—
His one clear eye watched diligently
His herd below
Of sheep and goats
Their bellies swelled
With sweetened grass—
His young but weathered face marred
By ancient tracery of cuts
Which stamped his tribe,
And saddened by that sightless,
                    marbled other-eye.
And now he raised his flute once more
To play a further tune—
The drifting, echoing notes took flight
Across the hills
And hit the paling sky
Where giant storks
Beat with their black-edged wings.

Lace Curtains

Through misted veil
She sees the street below
All ivoried
Breeze-moved, the scene is set
The busy boulangerie is there
And open now
The scents drift upward
Of fresh-baked bread and croissants
Morning-crisp —
While housewives hurry from the shop
With warm and elongated loaves
Beneath their arms.

She watches, as she's always done
Throughout the years
Her moving fingers on the fog of lace
Reflection of the patterned flowers
Against her age-cast face
Once beautiful,
But now marked out by memoried-living,
A face that has known love, long-past,
Perhaps too well.

She sees the modiste at the window
Opposite
Throw her a wave
And smile from pin-filled mouth
The ritual of a forty-year-span.
And sitting there
With grey hair neatly combed

Into a piled chignon
Shawled,
With carpet-slippered feet,
Warmed,
By ancient purring friend,
She watches life.

Direction: Seville

All along a chalk road
On a hot white day
Bleached bristled fields
Disappear on all sides;
She appears
Over the crest
Riding the white-dust surf
On tall-boned mule
With dappled greyhound prancing
At her side —
She laughs and raises her hand
As she passes and I see
That her eyes are blacker
Than the gleaming olives
In the bulging straw panniers.

17

Sandals

He has grown
In lands
Where sandals polish stone;
Where shadowed palm trees

Etch their fronds
Against red skies;
Where hanging air
Holds a conglomerate
Of spice,
And incense meets
The lowering curtain of the night.
He has heard
The plaintive discord
Of the bell of goat,
The roaring chatter in the busy market place
The whining song of beggar with his cup;
The carried-call from mosiac minaret ...
The thousand thunders of the Orient.

The Child of the Wind

You are child of the wind
And the fields, Young Girl,
Yet already you become a woman
Of the darker orchards,
The sun is reflected in
Your gilt-touched skin,
And reiterated in the flickering
Amber of your eyes.
Dappled, like gold-flaked pools,
Those eyes mirror
The innocence of your childhood:
The child you are,
And always will remain,
And the shadowed woman you begin to be.

I Know Your Love

Wild Call

"I am yours," breathed the wind
Warm as it came to me
Carrying the scents of all it had passed
On its way
Spicy perfume of wild thyme blending
⠀⠀⠀⠀⠀⠀⠀with pine and rose
And the sun, breaking suddenly from cloud
Beat its message, too, against my skin,
"I am yours!"

From the river rushed the water-call
Down its ever-tumbling fall of spray,
"I belong to you...to you!" it said.
And I heard my voice rising high
Lifted by an urgent force
Swelling to a shout
Which filled my lungs with air
And rent the wilderness
As I cried with open heart,
"I am yours!"
And all around they knew.

Winter Things

Better not to speak of grey and winter things
But cast them whispered to the wind
And freeze the pain of thoughts
Beneath the glassy, covered pond
Until the thaw of spring begins.
And when the first bud shines
Small-white upon the bough
Tremulous, you will breathe
                    the early air again
And touch softly at the hidden hurt that was.
With seeking fingers, you will find, that
Like the winter things, the pain
                    has crept away.

The Vine

Year upon year
Gentle tendrils
Began their spread
The frail twisting fibres
Grew thick and strong.
Now the vine is heavy;
Now the grapes are filled
With captured sun—
Vineyard of compassion
Weighed by the harvest
Of bitter summers and nutured by tears
Yet now the fruit is fullsome and sweet!

The Harvest Years

How many times have I told you of my love
In these September years we've shared?
You came to me in harvest time of life,
You brought me harvest gifts.
Gift of love mettled to endure
By furnaced years of suffering
By years deprived of love.

You brought me joy — a joy to share
Made more vital by the joyless years
All gone before.

You brought me tenderness, my love,
A tenderness that melts my heart.
Regret . . .
For years we did not share,
The painful spring and summer lived apart.
But harvest time is best
Its mellowed riches fill the soul,
And I must tell you often of my love
In these shared autumn years.

Now I have known

I think I did not truly come alive
Until I knew this gentleness
Sunlight on a seabird's wing
Blossom on the dogwood tree
Awareness of so many joys
All came to me

Again
More valued than they ever were before
Because I know your love.

And when you spill the words
Long-locked within your heart
Like fortune of a king
From guarded treasury
These sacred whispered words
Fall on my ears alone
I know, then, I could not
Live on long without your love.

As Driftwood

Each life is shaped by fate
As driftwood by the tides
As trees bent leaning to the winds
Rocks smoothed or edged by elements
Sculptured by nature across all time
Unmoulded by us, a shape is formed
And we, unknowing, modify the shape
Smooth down some jagged edge
*   with a patient acceptance*
Polish gravelled surfaces with gentleness
Or rend, in despair, a given ugliness
*   to some more weird cast*
And even sometimes, achieving with greatness,
*   beauty out of ugliness.*
Sometimes, in shame, destroying
*   what was once beautiful*
Or, in fear, allowing time's verdigris

to cover qualities
That lie unused because we know not
what they are.

Day to Remember

When striped sea bass were sizzling
                    on the coals
And sharpening wind stirred up the fading
                    evening air
Sun-soaked, sea-drenched, salt-dry
Our faces tingled
Whipped to a new-born youth by happiness.
And as the sun sank into the sea
Turning the blue to brazen gold,
We laughed together in a sudden welling joy
And wrote the date with fishy fingers
In the sand
To mark it in our memories.

The Gentle Argonaut

We found it together   23
A treasure on the sands
Swept across oceans
Beaten onto the beach
By giant breakers
Crushing in their fury all the hardier shells
They left the frail nautilus.
It lay pristine,
Untouched by oil,

Its virgin whiteness gleaming in the sun
Around it tangled green and scarlet weeds
Lay corrupted in a mass of tar.
We wondered as we held it
How its delicate beauty had remained intact
So fine the light shone through
This sculptured masterpiece
We marvelled at the Artist's hand
As we held the gentle argonaut.

The Thread of the Web

Running through the moving
Shadows of the trees
I find elation
In the silk of wind...
My half-discarded youth
Restored
I am no longer self
But creatured in the verdure
Of these sylvan woods
At one with bird;
With furred
And feathered things;
With sunlight dappling
On the deepened moss,
With resin seeped
Slow-glittered from the bark,
With scent of turf
And heat-dried fern...
I am at one with God!